Librarians/
Bibliotecarios

By Jacqueline Laks Gorman

Reading consultant: Susan Nations, M.Ed., author/literacy coach/consultant

Gareth Stevens
Publishing

Please visit our Web site www.garethstevens.com. For a free color catalog of all our high-quality books, call toll free 1-800-542-2595 or fax 1-877-542-2596.

Cataloging Data

Gorman, Jacqueline Laks, 1955-
    Librarians / Bibliotecarios by Jacqueline Laks Gorman.
      p. cm. — (People in my community)
    Summary: A simple introduction to the work of librarians in a library. Bilingual Edition.
    Includes bibliographical references and index.
    ISBN: 978-1-4339-3760-6 (pbk.)
    ISBN: 978-1-4339-3761-3 (6-pack)
    ISBN: 978-1-4339-3759-0 (library binding)
    1. Librarians—Juvenile literature. 2. Libraries—Juvenile literature.
  [1. Librarians. 2. Occupations. 3. Libraries. 4. Spanish-language materials] I. Title.

New edition published 2010 by
Gareth Stevens Publishing
111 East 14th Street, Suite 349
New York, NY 10003

New text and images this edition copyright © 2010 Gareth Stevens Publishing

Original edition published 2003 by Weekly Reader® Books
An imprint of Gareth Stevens Publishing
Original edition text and images copyright © 2003 Gareth Stevens Publishing

Art direction: Haley Harasymiw, Tammy Gruenewald
Page layout: Michael Flynn, Katherine A. Goedheer
Editorial direction: Kerri O'Donnell, Diane Laska Swanke
Spanish translation: Eduardo Alamán

Cover, back cover, p. 1 © Digital Vision/Getty Images; pp. 5, 7, 11, 15, 17, 19, by Gregg Andersen; pp. 9, 13, 21 © Shutterstock.com.

Printed in the United States of America

CPSIA compliance information: Batch #WW10GS: For further information contact Gareth Stevens, New York, New York at 1-800-542-2595.

Table of Contents

- -

Contenido

Boldface words appear in the glossary/
Las palabras en **negrita** aparecen en el glosario

Meet the Librarian

A librarian has an important job.
A librarian helps people.

Conoce a los bibliotecarios

Los bibliotecarios tienen un trabajo importante. Los bibliotecarios ayudan a las personas.

A librarian works in the library. A library has many books you can read.

Los bibliotecarios trabajan en las bibliotecas. Las bibliotecas tienen muchos libros que puedes leer.

A Librarian's Day

A librarian decides what books to buy for the library.

El día de un bibliotecario

Los bibliotecarios deciden qué libros se compran para la biblioteca.

The librarian puts the books on the **shelves**. Each book has to go in the right place.

Los bibliotecarios ponen los libros en los **estantes**. Cada libro tiene que estar en el lugar adecuado.

shelves/
estantes

11

Sometimes the librarian
uses a computer to answer
your questions.

- - - - - - - - - - - - - - - - - - - -

A veces, los bibliotecarios
usan computadoras para
contestar tus preguntas.

computer/
computadora

13

The librarian can help you find the book you want.

Los bibliotecarios te ayudan a encontrar el libro que buscas.

So Many Books!

The librarian can help you get a **library card**. Then you can take a book home!

¡Tantos libros!

Los bibliotecarios te ayudan a sacar una **tarjeta de la biblioteca**. ¡Así, puedes llevar libros prestados a tu casa!

library card/
tarjeta de la
biblioteca

17

The librarian checks out all your books. She tells you when to bring them back.

Los bibliotecarios te ayudan a sacar libros prestados de la biblioteca. Ellos te dicen cuándo hay que devolverlos.

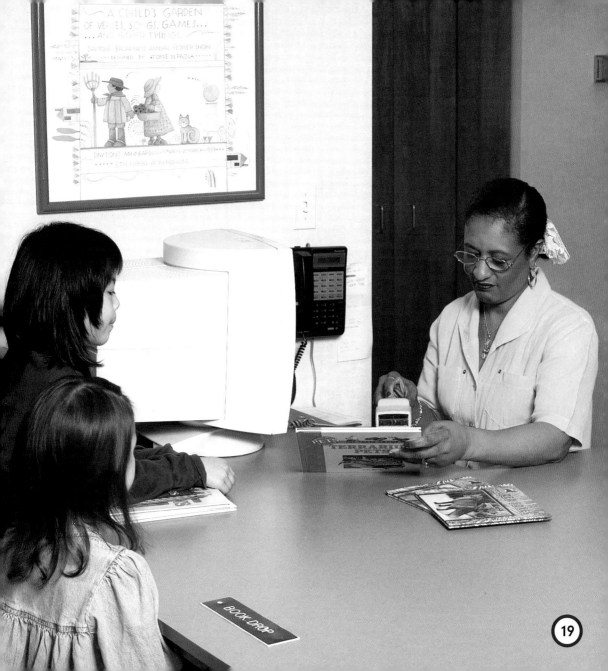

It looks like fun to be a librarian! Would you like to be a librarian?

Ser bibliotecario parece divertido. ¿Te gustaría ser bibliotecario?

Glossary/Glosario

library card: a special card
that is used to check things out of a library

shelves: thin pieces of wood or metal that hold books

----

estantes (los) piezas delgadas de metal o madera en
las que se ponen libros

tarjeta de la biblioteca (la) una tarjeta especial que se
usa para sacar libros de las bibliotecas.

For More Information/Más información

Books/Libros

Rau, Dana Meachen. *Librarians/Los bibliotecarios*. Marshall Cavendish, 2007

Ready, Dee. *Bibliotecarios y bibliotecarias*. Capstone Press, 1998

Web Sites/Páginas en Internet

Community Club: Librarian
http://teacher.scholastic.com/commclub/librarian/index.htm

Index/Índice

About the Author

Jacqueline Laks Gorman is a writer and editor. She grew up in New York City and began her career working on encyclopedias and other reference books. Since then, she has worked on many different kinds of books. She lives with her husband and children, Colin and Caitlin, in DeKalb, Illinois.

Información sobre la autora

Jacqueline Laks Gorman es escritora y editora. Jacqueline creció en la ciudad de Nueva York donde comenzó su carrera trabajando en enciclopedias y libros de referencia. Desde entonces ha trabajado en muchos libros infantiles. Jacqueline vive con su esposo y sus hijos, Colin y Caitlin, en DeKalb, Illinois.

Lavenia McCoy
Public Library

Pine River Library District

P.O. Box 227
395 Bayfield Center Drive
Bayfield, CO 81122
(970) 884-2222

www.lmpl.org